The
Stopsley
Picture
Book

BY JAMES DYER

For Ann

First Published November 1999
by
The Book Castle,
12 Church Street,
Dunstable,
Bedfordshire LU5 4RU

© James Dyer, 1999

The right of James Dyer to be identified as the Author
of this work has been asserted by him in accordance with
the Copyrights, Designs and Patents Act 1988.

ISBN 1 871199 948

Typeset by the Author.
Printed in Great Britain by Redwood Books,
Trowbridge, Wiltshire.

Contents

A Century of Stopsley

Acknowledgements

So many people have helped to make this book possible, by searching through their albums and rummaging through boxes in their lofts. It gives me great pleasure to thank them all.

As in my previous book, *The Stopsley Book*, a few people have given me especial help. First and foremost I must thank Myrtle Cox and Barbara Peters, who have provided pictures and answered many questions, or found the answers for me, often at the most inconvenient times. Particular thanks are due to Mary Hall and her daughter Susan Tarn for giving me free access to William Lockey's splendid photographs of Ramridge End. Once again I have drawn on *The Luton News* photographs stored at Luton Museum, and I am indebted to Chris Grabham of the Museum staff for making prints and the Editor, John Buckledee for allowing me to publish some of them.

These pictures have accumulated over thirty years, and if I have inadvertently failed to acknowledge anyone, I unreservedly apologise. I am most grateful for the help of all the following in providing me with photographs, information or advice:

ABC Television; Revd. David Alexander; Barbara Benson; Maureen Bland; Ann Boddy; John Burke; Eric Cannon; Basil Cheverton; Leslie Church; Mrs J.R.Clutterbuck; Kath. Crampton; Josie Driscoll; Frederick Dyer; Richard Everitt; Kevan Fadden; Patricia Faulkner; Norman Fisher; Eileen Flecknoe; Alan Gibbs; Shiela Gilley; Win Haines; The *Herald and Post*; Tilly Hodgson; the late Walter Lawrence; the staff of Luton Museum; *The Luton News*; Harold Maddick; Mick Marsh; Eric Meadows; Ray Miller; Ken Munslow; Norman Nash; Bob and Paddy Norman; Colin Nye; Freda Pinney; Jeanne Powell; Walter R. Rainbow; Richard Savage; David Scrimshire; Betty Shaw; John Shaw; Lionel Shaw; Ann Smith; Geoff Smith; Stuart Smith; Hillary Stubbs; Alan Thayne; the late Ethel Toyer; Trevor Tween; Ronald Walker; Fay Weighell; Mary Wilson; Marjorie Williamson; Keith Woods.

Introduction

The arrival of the 20th century seems to have passed with little celebration in Stopsley. Those who had calendars would have been aware of its significance, as would the people who could afford the luxury of a newspaper, but there was, of course, no radio or television to inflate the importance of the occasion. Queen Victoria was still on her throne, the British Empire was still the greatest ever, and the only blot on the landscape was the Boer War, half a world away in South Africa! Four Stopsley men were serving in the War at that time, Alfred Plummer, William Waller and Sydney Whittemore from Bury Road, and Private Wilson of Stopsley Common. Lieut. Thomas Sowerby of Putteridge Bury had returned from the Cape on 5th December and had been given a hero's welcome by the Stopsley School children.

There is no indication that the Revd. Arthur Love held any special Services at St Thomas' Church on Sunday, 31st December 1899. Six parishioners took Holy Communion at 8.15 am. Sunday School at 10.15 am and again at 2.30 pm had a fair attendance, as did the adult services at 11.00 am and 6.30 pm. There had been no New Year holiday for most of the men and boys who shivered as they worked on the local farms: the animals still had to be fed and the cows milked. The weather was decidedly chilly, only 3 degrees centigrade indoors, when School closed for Christmas on 21st December. There was the usual children's party, attended by Asher Hucklesby, the Mayor of Luton, and his wife. It was no warmer when term began again on 8th January 1900, with teachers suffering from influenza. The School Log Book, usually very informative, fails to tell us what special centenary lessons were taught. Headmaster, Charles Breed, never slow to miss a trick, would certainly not have missed such a golden opportunity. When the Parish Council met on Tuesday 9th January their main business was to accept the District Council's plans for supplying water to the village. Improvements to the surface of the High Street (Hitchin Road) would be deferred until the water mains had been laid. Once the meeting had concluded, the Chairman, Mr John Impey, entertained the members and their wives to a hot supper.

And so our village entered the most dramatic century in its history.

This is essentially a picture book of Stopsley in the 20th century. In 1900 photographs were, for the most part, still a novelty. The majority of pictures were either made in a studio, or by travelling professional photographers. They were usually taken to record beautiful scenery or architecture, a special event, a person or group of people. In Stopsley the earliest pictures were of the Church Sunday School teachers of 1881 and 1898, and the celebrations for Queen Victoria's Diamond Jubilee in 1897 (see *The Stopsley Book*, 1998). In this volume devoted to the 20th century, the pictures become more prolific as the century progresses, and photography more commonplace.

A travelling photographer visited the village school in 1901 to record the school children and teachers in their different classes. His camera, using slow glass plates, caught the simple dignity as well as the poverty of his subjects with penetrating clarity. By 1914, when the new village school was open, the groups were perhaps a little more formal, with each boy and girl wearing their Sunday best clothes.

The advent of the Brownie box camera in America in 1900 meant that very soon a new hobby became available to the masses, though its arrival in Stopsley was somewhat delayed. The earliest snap-shots that have survived date from the 1920s, with the work of the young school teacher Ethel Toyer, who delighted in photographing her family and friends at Stopsley and Round Green. Ethel's pictures also included her holidays and excursions to Hunstanton and Cambridge, camping with the Girl Guides, and a few rather poignant pictures of the graves of young pupils she had known. It is sad that her camera did not have a sharper lens.

William Lockey lived in a bungalow at 205 Ashcroft Road, (now demolished) opposite the junction with Turners Road, and at the entrance to Ramridge End Farm, where his wife's parents lived. Photography fascinated him, and using a good-quality camera taking 2¼ by 3¼ inch negatives, he pictured the farm and its surroundings, again and again, in all seasons and weathers, between 1925 and 1940. Many of his pictures were submitted to the Luton and District Camera Club annual exhibitions. Fortunately a number of his negatives have survived, although not always in a good condition.

South Bedfordshire was lucky in having a progressive local newspaper that made use of photographs throughout the century. The *Luton News* built up an impressive pictorial record of events in Stopsley and the surrounding district. Thousands of negatives, on glass and film, have survived and are stored at Luton Museum. Sadly, quite a lot more have been destroyed, and it is with fingers crossed that one searches through the files, hoping that a particular shot still exists. Fortunately many Stopsley folk bought copies of the *Luton News* pictures at the time they were taken, so it has sometimes been possible to find original prints from negatives since destroyed.

Some of the pictures in this volume show buildings and events that have long since passed into history. Within days of *The Stopsley Book* being published, the three photographs of *Ivy Cottage* appeared. This large and attractive house stood at the centre of the village, close to the War Memorial, and unknown to anyone under seventy years of age. What an historic feature it would have been, had it survived. Similarly, *Tithe Cottage* was frequently photographed, but with a lack of preservation laws and funds for restoration, it was largely destroyed by the middle of the century, and is now just a picture-postcard memory.

Stopsley folk stare at us from a Methodist Chapel gathering (plate 49). The names of the majority are committed to oblivion. With the records of the Chapel missing, its seems unlikely that we will ever discover who they were, unless someone somewhere has a named copy of the photograph.

A pencil sketch by Harold Maddick of the junction of Wigmore Lane (left) and Ashcroft Road about 1950. The cottages in the centre have been replaced by the Wigmore Lane Garage. The gas-lamp standards stood at roughly 120 metre intervals. They burnt coal-gas piped from Luton, and were operated manually by a lamplighter who travelled on a bicycle until 1939. After the War and five years of blackout, they were adapted to turn on automatically.

The great tragedy with most old photographs is that their owners frequently failed to date and name them. The author has spent days trying to identify people, or to trace an event and give it a date. Even newspaper photographs didn't always get published, and when they did, it can often take hours of searching through back numbers in an effort to identify the exact event. I would plead with everyone who has family or local pictures to name and date them whilst they still remember who and what they show. Don't put it off till the dark winter evenings. Do it whilst it is fresh in your mind. Make sure that your senior relatives identify as many of the oldest pictures as possible before it is too late, otherwise they will become useless as primary evidence for the study of local and family history

The Stopsley Book
Some Additions and Corrections

Since *The Stopsley Book* was published in 1998 some additional information and corrections have become available, and are discussed below.

Bury Farm, formerly in St Thomas' Road, where the new Baptist Church now stands, seems to have had a number of names in the past. Bleak Hall Farm and Stopsley Farm have been noted. In a deed of 1683 there is a record of John Rickett living in Nooks Farm at Stopsley, and the Catalogue of a Sale at the George Hotel in Luton on 30th July 1846 refers to Noaks Farm. The description in the latter makes it quite clear that Noaks or Nooks Farm and Bury Farm are one and the same establishment, and that 1846 would have been the year when it was acquired by the Pigott family. Incidentally, anyone wishing to view the property at that time was invited to contact Levi Welch of Stopsley. In 1867 Welch was charged with highway robbery.

The same Sale Catalogue describes Dancer's Farm, at the foot of Bradgers Hill, as 'a four-roomed brick and slated foreman's cottage, two-bay barn, stables, sheds, poultry house, enclosed yard, rickyard, etc.' Bradgers Hill is referred to as Bradshaw's Hill Common. I am indebted to Mr Geoffrey Smith for drawing my attention to this catalogue.

There are a number of references to the Boulter family in *The Stopsley Book*. It is now clear that Jesse Bolter and his children, who lived at Pond Farm, spelt their surname without a 'u'.

On page 106 of *The Stopsley Book* the name of Ernest Chamberlain appears in the list of men who died in the First World War. This is incorrect. He died in 1941, during the Second World War, at the hands of the Japanese. His name appears correctly on page 114 of the same book.

In plate LXb the sixth bell ringer is Robert Perry, not Ronald. Tragically, Robert died, aged 15½, shortly after this picture was taken.

1 *Ivy Cottage* stood on what is now the car-park of the S and K Superstore in Hitchin Road, almost opposite the War Memorial.   This photograph was taken in February 1915 when the left side was the home of Edith Fisher and her children Norman, Ena and baby Ethelbert James.   Fred (Titty) Tufnell lived in the right hand side of the house. A Sale Catalogue of June 1910 describes the property as 'two brick stucco and tiled Cottages now occupied by Mrs Harris and Mr James Tufnell, at rents producing £10 per annum.   Each Cottage contains 2 Rooms downstairs and 2 up.   There are 2 Barns and 1 Privy. Outgoings: Vicarial Tithe, 3 pence.'   *(Josie Driscoll)*

2   A wider view of *Ivy Cottage*.   The lion crest above the front door indicates that it was built by the Sowerby family of Putteridge Bury sometime around 1820.   The Sowerby's held much of the land in Stopsley in the 19th century.   The house stood end-on to the Hitchin Road: the barns to the right would now be in the school playground.   The village War Memorial can just be seen to the left of the house.   *(Josie Driscoll)*

3   The last occupants of *Ivy Cottage* were William Fisher and his family.   William was an enthusiastic rose grower and sold rose buds for gentlemens' lapels at 6 pence (3p.) each   As a result he was known in the village as 'Bud' Fisher.   The house was demolished around 1930.   *(Josie Driscoll)*

4 *Tithe Cottage* in the 1920s. It stood near the roundabout on the site of the Barratt's building. Between 1870 and 1890 part of it was a private school run by Georgina Menlove, assisted by John Stevens who had at one time been the headmaster of the Board School at Swift's Green. *Tithe Cottage* was certainly older than *Ivy Cottage*. It was of timber frame construction with brick filling below and lath and plaster above. *(Arthur Allen)*

5 *Tithe Cottage* about 1920, when it was still safe to drive sheep and cattle along the Hitchin Road. In the distance a motor cycle proceeds towards *Elm House* (671 Hitchin Road). *Elm House* is one of Stopsley's two allegedly haunted houses. The ghost of a small 'animal' was claimed to have been seen by former residents, only one of whom found it threatening. *(Author's Collection)*

6 This composite photograph gives an impression of the cottages that lined the south side of Hitchin Road, in the centre of the village, about 1925. Jabez Cook's grocery shop, later the Post Office, is hidden behind the lady. The cottage (above the man's hat) became A.E.Fisher's butchers shop. The last house on the left, standing end-on to the village Green, is *Virginia Cottage*. The photographs were taken in Venetia Road on the site of the future Henderson's Newsagents. The man was Horace Roberts, a shoe repairer. *(Ethel Toyer)*

7 *Virginia Cottage* stood end-on to the road on the south side of the Green, close to the point where the dual carriageway from Luton joins the traffic roundabout. The cottage was once covered with Virginia creeper, hence its name. It had an extensive vegetable garden at the rear, and a well to provide its own water supply. The lady is possibly Mrs Mardle. A notice in the window, not quite legible, appears to advertise boot and shoe repairs. *(Ethel Toyer)*

8 The western corner of St Thomas' Road and Lothair Road about 1970.   On the right is Eveling's drapers shop selling 'clothing, household linen and shoes for all the family'.   The small bungalow next door was demolished to allow the shop to expand.   Reginald Rainbow occupied number 14.   Beyond can be seen the Church Institute demolished in 1973, and the roof of the old Baptist Church.   The gas lamp on the corner reminds us that street lighting in Stopsley first appeared in 1923.   *(Walter R. Rainbow)*

9   The eastern corner of Lothair Road and St Thomas' Road in 1993.   This shop was originally built in the 1930s to mirror that in the plate above.   It had a varied existence, having been the second Stopsley Branch Library, a fish-and-chip shop and turf accountants. It served its final years as an estate agents, before demolition in 1994.   To its right stood Wally Lawrence's shoe repair shop and *The Sportsman* public house.   *(James Dyer)*

10 Hitchin Road about 1956.   On the right Green Farm has been replaced by a succession of garages, including Stopsley Motor Services, selling Esso petrol.   The grocery chain of W. H. Cullen had a branch in the building now occupied by the HSBC (Midland) Bank   R. A. Hopkins Ltd., chemists, had been next door since 1936.   Cecil Halsey's hairdressing salon is prominently advertised.   The corner shop is Stan Toyer's hardware stores.   Beyond the telephone kiosk was Ball and Parish, newsagents and confectioners.   More shops and private houses follow before the Wesleyan Methodist Church with its turret is seen.   Beyond is the War Memorial and houses in St Thomas' Road, since demolished.   *(Mason's Alpha Series)*

11 It is hard to believe that this is the busy northern end of Ashcroft Road, taken about 1925, looking towards the cottages on the Green.   The photographer probably stood close to the future entrance to the Recreation Ground (near 56 Ashcroft Road).   At that time the road was known as Ramridge End Lane.   The Stopsley Greyhound Track, which appeared briefly in 1929-30, lay behind the hedge on the right.   *(Ethel Toyer)*

12 Looking east over Ashcroft Road from the Fire Station (1989).   Hazelwood Close and Hawthorn Avenue are in the middle distance, with Elderberry Close (on the old Vicarage site) on the extreme left.   The trees of Putteridge Park are on the skyline beyond.   The gardens in the foreground were once part of Bolter's Meadow.   *(James Dyer)*

13 The prettification of the Green had begun by 1948 with the introduction of flower beds. *Tithe Cottage* (centre left) has become Greenways Café and garage. The barn occupied by Stopsley Working Mens' Club is behind the fence (centre) On the right is the Police Box with emergency telephone. This was the bus terminus for some years. The tall pole carried the air raid siren throughout the 1939-45 War. Tall standards with sodium lamps replace the old gas lamps. *(Luton News: Luton Museum Collection)*

14 The 33rd Luton (Stopsley) Cub Scout Pack parading in 1952 in front of *Jutland House*. The house was built in 1916 and became the home of school teacher Maud Hucklesby. In 1954 it was acquired by R. W. Warner and converted into a shop. For twenty years it was the village Post Office. Today, with an extension on the left, it is a video shop. On the right is the home of the Wells family, and *Ivy Cottage* stood beyond. *(Bob Norman)*

15 and 16   The death knell for Stopsley as a village was sounded in 1959 when building began on Jansel House, the headquarters of the building firm, H. C. Janes Ltd.   It replaced the diminutive Pond Farm which stood to the right of the new building, at the end of Putteridge Road.   Most of Jansel House was built in Pond Meadow (see plate 30) and *Tithe Cottage* stood at the northern (left) end.   In the upper picture the roofs of the new Working Mens' Club and the old Vicarage can be seen through the girders.   *(Basil Cheverton)*

17 In 1920, shortly after he was demobilised, Ted Simpkins constructed these glass houses on old allotments off the present Tancred Road. For the next forty years he provided high quality fresh salad and vegetable produce for the Stopsley district. *(Geoff. Smith)*

18 Although originally a builder by trade, Ted Simpkins nursery gardening skills led to his vegetable products being much sought after, particularly during the war years. Here he is pictured (left) with his niece, Connie Smith and his father, Charles Simpkins. *(Geoff. Smith)*

19 By 1933 Ted Simpkins had built his own greengrocer's shop at 603 Hitchin Road. This picture shows the window beautifully stocked with fresh fruit and vegetables. *(Geoff. Smith)*

20 The Post Office in Bury Road (St Thomas' Road) about 1920. The name of Percy Smith Kime appears above the door and below the gas lamp. Most of the shop sold groceries, but with a Post Office counter on the right. In the large house beyond the double gates lived Alfred Roberts, a carter. To the left of the Post Office was Mrs Burkett, with a bucket of fresh flowers for sale. The houses in the middle distance were condemned and demolished in the mid-1930s. *(Author's Collection)*

21 St John's Mission Church at Round Green began life as a Wesleyan Chapel. It was leased to St Thomas' church in 1914 as a chapel of ease for Round Green members. Following its closure in 1933 it had a varied career, being used for Civil Defence exercises during and just after the 2nd World War and housing the Stopsley and District Branch of the British Legion, which had formed in 1946. The building was demolished in the late 1950s, and its site is now a car park. *(Stuart Smith)*

22 St Thomas' Church Institute opened in January 1927, providing a much-needed venue for local gatherings. Land had been acquired ten years earlier, but it took many jumble sales, bazaars and raffles to raise the £906 needed to pay for its construction. It was demolished in 1973 when it became a health hazard. *(Ethel Toyer)*

23 St Francis' Church in Carteret Road was consecrated on 13th February 1960 to serve the needs of the Ashcroft and Vauxhall areas. Although this part of Stopsley was originally in St Thomas' ecclesiastical parish, it had by 1960 transferred to St Mary's, Luton. It became a separate parish in 1977. The building was designed by the architects Peter Dunham, Widdup and Harrison of Union Street, Luton. *(Eric Meadows)*

24 St Thomas' Church (1992) was consecrated on 2nd June 1862 by the Bishop of Rochester. It was designed by H. J. Pearson, a Luton architect, and built at a cost of £1,150. A new porch was added in 1983. The first burial in the churchyard was that of Emma Dimmock, a baby of 15 months, in August 1862. By 1940 the graveyard was ostensibly full, and most new burials were transferred to the Crawley Green Road cemetery. The Vale cemetery opened in 1954, followed by the Crematorium six years later. *(James Dyer)*

25 1962, when this aerial view was taken, was a time of rapid transition for Stopsley. Dwarfing *Tithe Cottage*, the new *Jansel House* was merely a year old. The Hitchin Road was the main artery through the old village centre. Work had already begun on the dual carriageway from Hitchin that would cut the village in half by 1967-8. Prominent on the left of the picture are the Wesleyan Church and *The Sportsman*, with Lawrence's shoe repair shop to their right. R. A. Hopkins warehouse and the garage workshop dominate the centre of the picture. The old houses in Hitchin Road (plate 6) have not yet been demolished, but the new public toilets are complete. The football pitches at the new Stopsley Sports Centre are in place, though an area of old allotments has still to be reclaimed. In the background the Vale Cemetery (1954) and Crematorium (1960) are still in a formative stage of development. *(Luton News: Luton Museum Collection)*

26 By 1994 when this picture was taken above St Thomas' Road, the new Baptist Church was about to be opened. Together with Mixes Hill Court, they stood on the site of Bury Farm. The Municipal Caravan Site (1963) was constructed over the filled-in clay pits of the St Thomas' Road brickworks. During the two World Wars the flooded clay pits were used by the military for manoeuvres, and the local children for fishing. The Ashcroft Road Recreation Ground is clearly visible at the top of the picture. *(Herald and Post Newspapers)*

27 Little has changed in this picture of Manor Farm since it was taken about 1920. This is Luton's only surviving working farm. In 1871 the Sowerby Estate, which owned the farm employed 27 men and 9 boys to work 1,005 acres. Today farmer Lionel Shaw and one man manage 876 acres of land at both Manor and Whitehill Farms. *(John Shaw)*

28 In 1886 George Shaw was the first member of his family to acquire the tenancy of Manor Farm. His brother, Charles Hugh Shaw from Whitwell took it over from 1902 until his death in 1934. Charles Hugh is seen here with his wife Mary Cecil (née Simons) The Simons farmed at Annables Farm, Kingsbourne Green. Charles Hugh Shaw was a member of the Parish Council for four years, and assisted the Fire Brigade in endeavouring to extinguish the Luton Town Hall fire following the riots of 19th-20th July 1919. *(Lionel Shaw)*

29   This damaged snapshot shows the shepherd Frederick Brazier working with his large herd of sheep and lambs on the hilltop near Whitehill Farm.   His son Walter died at Ypres on 31st July, 1917.   On the original print it is just possible to make out the outline of Warden Hill on the right skyline.   *(Walter R. Rainbow)*

30   Bolter's herd of dairy cattle resting in Pond Meadow beside Pond Farm, where Jansel House now stands.   The outbuildings of *Tithe Cottage* can be seen in the orchard on the left in this pastoral view of 1930.   *(Author's Collection)*

31 Home Farm, Putteridge Bury about 1925. The farmhouse and its outbuildings were built to the designs of the Scottish landscape architect, John Claudius Loudon, who had laid out the grounds of the Bury after the disastrous fire of 1808. The dovecote is in the same style, and is almost certainly later than the date of 1788 suggested by Jean Taylor and quoted in *The Stopsley Book*. Loudon is better known for designing the model village of Great Tew in Oxfordshire. *(William Lockey)*

32 The drawing room of Putteridge Bury house after the rebuild of 1911, with furnishings specially designed to match. The long refectory table is still in the house. A feature of this room was the 16th century stained glass, mostly of unknown continental origin, that had been inlaid in the windows. *(Mrs J. R. Clutterbuck)*

33 Snow on Stopsley Common during the harsh winter of 1947. This view from 60 Bradgers Hill Road shows Stopsley Common Farm amongst the trees in the centre. Just visible beyond is Waterhall Farm, with haystacks to the left. The isolated house beside the Old Bedford Road is West View Beneath the snow on the left can be seen the outlines of Bushmead Road and Fairford Avenue, and the fence of Luton Grammar School. This corner of the school field was used for growing potatoes during the War. In the foreground are the lynchets, virtually scrub free, and used for skiing in 1947. *(Win Haines)*

34 A haystack and farm wagon on Ramridge End Farm about 1930. It would be fascinating to know if the wagon was one that had belonged to the Barber family who farmed Ramridge End in the mid-19th century, and some of whose Account Books survive from between 1816 and 1837. Today Rickyard Close marks this spot. *(William Lockey)*

35 William Lockey was a talented amateur photographer who pictured Ramridge End Farm in all seasons between 1925 and 1940.   His wife Dora was the daughter of the farmer, John Holdstock.   This view looks east beyond the farmhouse towards the present day Mobley Green and Sowerby Avenue.   The meadow was permanent pasture providing grazing for cattle and sheep, with a pond just inside the gate.   *(William Lockey)*

36 A wintry view of the house about 1925, with the pond frozen over, but a convenient hole broken for the animals and ducks.   It seems likely that the farm originally consisted of two separate houses.   The left hand end without the creeper has a cellar beneath it, and dairies beyond.   (See 38).   *(William Lockey)*

37 By 1936 the western end of the farmhouse had been extended to provide a new kitchen and bedroom above. The pond beside the gate has been filled in as a safety precaution. There were a number of small children around the farm at that time. *(William Lockey)*

Farmyard

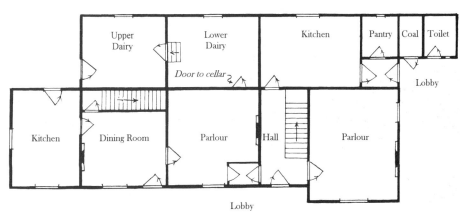

Front Garden

38 A groundfloor plan of Ramridge End Farm, compiled from memory by Marjorie Williamson (née Holdstock), daughter of the last farmer. All the buildings were demolished in 1952 to make way for the Ramridge housing estate. Steps descended into the Lower Dairy, from where a door led into a cellar below the Parlour.

39 The last occupants of Ramridge End Farm, the Holdstock family, with their friends in 1932. Farmer Fred Holdstock holds the horse, with his wife Ida beside him. On the extreme right is his mother, Perthaney. His father John stands with his granddaughter Anne Lockey. On his right is Gladys Burgess, with her husband Walter Burgess on the far left. Little Mary Lockey is between them. The seated ladies and child are unidentified. A Burgess family had farmed at Ramridge before the 1st World War. It is not known if Walter Burgess was related to it.   *(William Lockey)*

40 John and Perthaney Holdstock with their granddaughter Anne Lockey, feeding their free -range hens in 1932. There was a demand for farm eggs in the days before battery farming. If the farmer did not market his own eggs a higgler or egg dealer would purchase them from him, and sell them at the nearest market for a small profit.   *(William Lockey)*

41 The great aisled barn at Ramridge End was at least 300 years old. According to Joseph Barber's *Account Book* in 1835, pitch was bought to preserve all the woodwork. The high central doors would allow loaded wagons to be driven into the barn. As well as storage bays for sheaves, there would originally have been a threshing floor, later replaced by a threshing machine (see 43). In the background houses in Ashcroft Road encroach. *(William Lockey)*

42 William Lockey was always looking for exhibition pictures, and this carefully posed shot with members of his family at Ramridge End is no exception. *(William Lockey)*

43 Wheat was cut with a binder, tied into sheaves and placed in stooks to dry. It was then piled into stacks until threshing could begin. A small farm would hire its threshing machine from A.T. Oliver at Wandon End. Oliver would also supply a traction engine to power it. From the 1950s most farms owned or hired combine harvesters to cut and thresh their cereals in one operation. The workers in this picture, taken at Ramridge End about 1930, have not been identified *(William Lockey)*

44 Inside the great barn at Ramridge End with its tenoned rafters and brick-set floor. An accumulation of old sacks and a chaff-cutting machine contribute to a nostalgic smell that still lingers in the nostrils of folk who knew it fifty years ago. *(W. Lockey)*

45 In 1936 Luton Corporation bought Eaton Green Farm as the site for a municipal airport. They paid the farmers, Ben and William Hartop, £32,950. The farmhouse can be seen in in front of the hangers in this picture. To its right are the stables, utilised by the Luton Flying Club. This photograph was taken soon after the opening of the airport in July 1938 by the Rt. Hon. Sir Kingsley Wood, Secretary of State for Air. Stopsley village is in the distance with Warden Hill beyond. The white roads of the future Ramridge estate are clearly visible.

(Luton News: Luton Museum Collection)

46 The Mothers' Union was founded in 1876. It is not clear when it began in Stopsley though it may have grown out of the monthly Mothers' Meetings that were being held by 1910. This photograph was taken at the old vicarage about 1925. Standing in the *back row:* Mrs Ekins; Mrs Warner; Miss L. Hill; Mrs Mott; Mrs Whittemore; - ; Mrs Kime; Mrs Allen who made the banner; Mrs Langdale; Mrs Dawson; Mrs Toyer; Mrs Jepps; Mrs Davis; Mrs Bunker. *Middle row:* Miss S. Hill; Mrs Frost; Mrs Fitzjohn; Mrs Peters; Mrs Hillhouse; - ; Mrs Gilbert; Mrs Shaw; Mrs Bigmore; Mrs Brewer, Mrs Coleman with twins; Mrs E. Hill. *Front row:* Mrs Toyer; - ; Mrs Fisher; Mrs Bangs; Mrs Whitemore; Mrs Goodship; Mrs Armitage; Mrs Jepps; Mrs Bacon; Mrs Breed. *(Frederick Thurston)*

47 On Sunday 14th November 1920 the Revd. E. T. Leslie led the dedication of the village War Memorial. Only 24 names are inscribed upon it although some forty Stopsley men lost their lives in the conflict. In the background can be seen the old Baptist Chapel, Ted Simpkins' new greenhouses and some of the brickworks drying sheds. *(Author's Collection)*

48 When 37 years old Charles Burkett was buried on 16th April 1928 he was escorted from his house in Bury Road (St Thomas' Road) by fellow members of the Ancient Order of the Buffalo's. That was one of a number of philanthropic Friendly Societies that looked after the interests of members and their families in sickness, infirmity and poverty, and amongst other things paid burial expenses, all in exchange for a small weekly contribution. Burkett had distinguished himself in the retreat from Mons in August 1914. The houses on the left were built by C. T. Webb about 1890 and demolished in the 1950s. *(Kath Crampton)*

49 Members of the Stopsley Wesleyan Methodist Church gathered for a Treat about 1915: the venue is unknown. Amongst Stopsley families represented are the Smiths, Cains, Kimes and Summerfields. In front of the marquee in the trilby hat is Mr Tichmarsh the Sunday School teacher. Next but one to him is Sarah Brazier. Her sons Fred and Walter are 1st and 3rd in the back row. Walter died at Ypres in 1917. *(Geoff. Smith)*

50 In June 1929 it was the turn of St Thomas' Church to entertain the Diocesan Lay Helpers Association. This picture shows them assembled on the old vicarage lawn in Putteridge Road. The Parochial Church Council minute book records that ladies from the parish catered for the occasion. *(Author's Collection)*

51 An informal snapshot of members of the Stopsley Mothers' Union with their infants assembling for a photograph in the vicarage garden about 1928. *(Geof. Smith)*

52 The tradition of parish tea makers has continued for years in Stopsley. Teams of ladies have willingly and without financial reward regularly prepared teas for older members of the community. Stalwarts in the 1950s and 60s were Gladys Clarke, Elsie Stangroom, Violet Bunyan and Edith Fisher, pictured here in the Church Institute. *(Author's Collection)*

53 During the incumbency of the Revd. Denby Gilbert (1922-38) numerous dramatic and musical entertainments were produced by his wife Winifred. This picture from about 1930 shows the cast of a show with a Japanese theme. It was taken in the present Stopsley Infant School playground.

54 Stopsley folk loved fancy clothes and were always dressing up. This group was pictured where St Thomas' Court now stands, sometime in the early 1930s. *(Author's Collection)*

55 The Church Sunday School Fancy Dress Parade of 1929 passing Pond Farm, on its way from the Institute to the Vicarage.   The adults are Winifred Blake (right) and Rita Miller (centre, with Kath and Freda Miller dressed as flower fairies).   The Bolter family are watching from behind the farm fence.   *(Luton News: Luton Museum Collection)*

56 For the Church Fête of 1938 Frank Bolter and his sister Mary became Highway 'men' and demanded a ransom for charity. Mrs Edith Fisher and her daughter Josie do not seem to mind being challenged.   *(Josie Driscoll)*

57 Stopsley ladies were always on the lookout for a novelty stall at the church fête. On this occasion handkerchiefs are the attraction, and the sales ladies are Gladys Clarke, Mary Hare and Violet Bunyan. The customer is Phylis Clarke, wife of J. G. R. Clarke, the local G.P.

58 Winifred Gilbert got this idea for a Sunday School children's' entertainment after a visit to the circus in 1932. The white horses are (*back row*) Vera Marlow, Thelma Hayward, Zena Marlow, Muriel Fisher, Amy Crick, Barbara Peters, (*kneeling*) Patricia Armstrong, Elsie Whittemore, Phylis Tingey. The Ringmaster is Stanley Conisbee, with brother Gordon behind him. The clowns are (*left*) Ray Miller and (*right*) Tom Catlin (?). *(Luton News)*

59 Yet another childrens' fancy dress parade, this time in 1946.   Although the War had only just ended there was little sign of austerity in the design of the costumes, which all represented fairy tale characters.

60 The Revd. Francis Estdale's first St Thomas' Church Fête in 1961.   His wife Marian and daughter Julie are in the vicarage garden beside him.   To the right are Mrs Reading and Mrs Wynd of the organising committee.

61   Stopsley Junior School playground was the venue for this fancy dress competition in 1944.   Amongst the participants are Mary Witney, Gillian Hodgson, Josie Fisher, Pamela Bierton, Ray Copley, William Howard and Tony Clayton.   The old *First and Last* can be seen in the background with Balderson's the Chemists (590 Hitchin Road) to the left.   The Library was not put up until 1948.   *(Luton News)*

62   The St Thomas' Church Sunday School class for 4-5 year olds in September 1947.   The teachers along the back row were Joan Gray, Edna Morris, Fay Fryer, Heather Jackson, Sheila Harman and Brenda Burgess.   *(Author's Collection)*

63 With the post-war growth of the Ramridge estate, Sunday School provision was urgently needed, and between April 1950 and September 1952 classes were held in the Ashcroft Café in Yeovil Road, led by Myrtle Cox. They later moved to Ramridge Infant School. *(M. Cox)*

64 St Thomas' Church Junior Sunday School tea party in 1947, with the Revd. H. T. Pimm helping to serve. Around the table from the left are David Scrimshire, Roy Perry, Isobel Allen, Gillian Hodgson, Robert Perry, Trevor Taylor, Mary Witney, Pauline Millard, Marie Thompson, Barry Morris, Brian Morris, - ,Christopher Fryer and David Clark. At the back are Mrs Walker and Mrs Fisher, - , - , Maureen Marsden, Janet Foreman, Ivan Lawrence and Tony Clayton. *(Luton News)*

65 A Christmas party at the Church Institute in 1946. It was the Revd. Pimm's first Christmas at Stopsley. The guest of honour was Ronald Alderson, Luton's last Chief Constable before the force was amalgamated into the Bedfordshire Constabulary in March 1947. Amongst others in the front of the picture are Mrs Burgess, Betty Bodsworth, Mrs Edith Fisher, Josie Fisher, Mrs Tilly Hodgson. *(Luton News)*

66 The Revd. Clifford Pollard's leaving party in the autumn of 1960. He left Stopsley to become Staff Padre with the Toc H in Kent. Local farmer and churchwarden, Pat Shaw, is on the extreme left. *(Luton News)*

67 The senior members of St Thomas' Church choir on a Whit Monday outing to Cambridge about 1909. It was arranged by the Revd. Walter Covey-Crump, who had strong links with the city. Harry Toyer (see plate 87) is on the extreme right, with William Hill, the sexton and verger for 46 years, sitting next to him. It is recorded that every Christmas before the 1st World War, the Choir, men and boys, performed a pantomime in the old School at Swift's Green. Miss Platt, who lived in Putteridge Road, laundered, starched and ironed their surplices for one shilling each (5p.). *(Author's Collection)*

68 A happy snapshot of the Revd. Mark Slater and Canon Francis Estdale. The Canon retired from St Thomas' Church in September 1994 after 33 years as incumbent. Revd. Slater was the Priest-in-charge of Bushmead Conventional District from 1993 till 1999 when he became Vicar of St Luke's Church, St Albans. *(Jim Gabriel)*

69 As part of its ongoing missionary work the Baptist Church held a Chinese Festival in 1942 in the Church Institute. Here are the participants, suitably dressed. In the back row, slightly right of centre, are the Revd. Alan Funnell and George Souster. *(Luton News)*

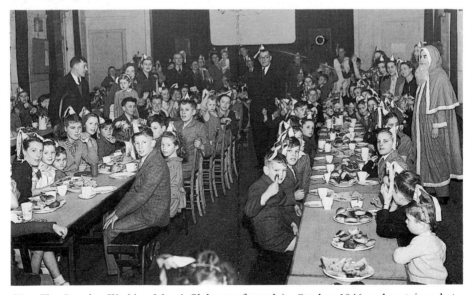

70 The Stopsley Working Mens' Club was formed in October 1946 and met in a hut adjoining the Greenways Café (where the Barratt building now stands). At Christmas 1947 they held a party for their children in the Junior School Hall. The youngsters were entertained by a conjuror and film show. *(Luton News)*

71 The St Thomas' Church Lads Brigade pictured in the vicarage garden in 1947. The boys in peaked caps from left to right: - , - , - , Bob Guess, - , Jack Fensome, Donald Hills, David Walker. Lads in forage caps: Fred Carman, Ronald Walker, Ivan Lawrence, Sam Warrington, Keith Blaxhill, Keith Worsley, - , Derrick York, Brian Bowles. Officers: WO. Ted Bradbury, Lt. Ray Miller, Capt. Staveley Knight, 2nd Lt. Ernie Hills. Front: Alec Kidd, John Dellar, - , Colin Bridges, Brian Morris, Brian Bailey, David Burgess.

72 According to surviving members this picture shows the 14th Luton (Stopsley) Girl Guide Company in 1921, which met in St John's Church at Round Green. The Guides Association claims to have no record of this Company. Guides identified : *Back row*: Eileen Bangs, - , - , Phyllis Fitzjohn, Mabel Dawson, Joyce Leslie, Ethel Flecknoe. *Centre*: Margaret Tansley, Capt. Cranfield, - , - , Gladys Dawson. *Front*: Doll Peters, - , Bertha Bunker.

(W. H. Cox)

73 By August 1925 Ethel Toyer had joined the Stopsley Guides, and took this snapshot of six of her friends at camp.

74 The 1st Stopsley Brownies on parade outside St Thomas' Church about 1942. Tilly Hodgson and Gladys Clements were in charge. *(Myrtle Cox)*

75 Stopsley and Biscot Church Lads' Brigade members outside Biscot Church, Trinity Road, Limbury in 1942. Amongst those parading for Stopsley are Sgt. Ray Miller, Geoff Smith, Len Tavener, Stan Waller, Jack Hendry, Colin Bridges, John Lowrie, Major Smith and Capt. Howe (with flag). *(Luton News)*

76   The 33rd Luton (Stopsley) Cub Scout pack, January 1952, at Stopsley High School. *Back row:* Rita Jarman (née Faulkner), Frances Norman (née Robson). *Centre:* John Watt, - , Robert Seaton, Peter Allen, Godfrey Taylor, Bobby Robinson, David Betts.   *Front:* Richard Patterson, - , Peter Hetherington, Dennis Hyde.   *(Bob Norman)*

77   Ross Park Spectaculars were held for some years to raise money for the Scout Movement.   Situated in Peartree Road, Ross Park was land given to the Scouts in 1962 by Leslie B. Sell.   An old prefabricated house from south Wales and a First World War army hut were erected on the site to provide a base for Scouting activities. *(Luton News: Luton Museum Collection)*

78 Children from Turners Road and central Ashcroft Road celebrating the Coronation of Queen Elizabeth II in June 1953 by taking part in a fancy dress parade at Ramridge School.

(Photocraft)

79 Happy children outside the doors of Stopsley Infant School in 1933. *Back row*: Winnie Bignall, Barbara Peters, - , Phylis Tingey. *Front row*: - , Iris Tuffnell, Grace Hemley, Margaret Whalley, and Margery Jones. Margaret Whalley was the daughter of the Senior School Headmaster.

(Barbara Peters)

80 "The Stopsley Baptist folk are such happy people, whenever they come out of church they are always smiling". In response to this remark, the whole congregation was photographed with the Revd. Norman Green outside the church one Sunday morning in the early 1970s. *(Echo and Post)*

81 With a rapidly increasing congregation, the Baptists urgently needed a new hall. Here John Norris and Pat Groom lead their fellow Sunday School members in a brick-laying ceremony. The completed hall was opened by Sir Herbert Janes in September 1954. *(Luton News)*

82 Music has always played an important part in the life of Stopsley Baptist Church. In 1951 the Junior Choir took part in an *Eistedfodd* at the Central Mission in Midland Road, Luton. Beryl Warby, their trainer, is at the piano. *(Luton News)*

83 A Nativity play was always a feature of the St Thomas' Christmas celebrations.   This performance took place in the Institute in 1951.   *(Luton News)*

84 The Stopsley Ladies' Lifeboat Guild was formed in November 1957.   During its first years it collected over £2,000 for the R.N.L.I.   The founder members celebrated its 10th birthday in November 1967 with a dinner at *La Casetta* in Guildford Street, Luton.   In the picture are *(L. to R.)* Mrs E. Howard, Mrs E. Fisher, Mrs P. Walker, Mrs R. Dyer, Mrs J. Ward, and Mrs P.E.Pinn.   The group thrives today as the Stopsley Lifeboat Branch, with both male and female members.   *(Luton News)*

85 Stopsley Girl Guides enjoying their somewhat frugal Christmas teaparty in 1947. Food was still rationed at that time. *(Luton News)*

86 Winter 1947 was the coldest of the 20th century. Temperatures stayed below freezing both day and night for most of January, with intermittent snow falling through February, and in March a great blizzard that created drifts up to 5 feet (2m.) high. The thick snow looked beautiful, but it caused many problems, particularly since Britain was still making a painful recovery from the War. Food and clothing were still rationed. There were great fuel shortages and frequent power cuts. Many Luton factories struggled to remain in production without any heating, and offices and shops tried to work by candlelight. But for children the excitement of snowball fights and sliding far outweighed the disadvantages. This picture shows Bradgers Hill road. The author recalls sitting on his school satchel and tobogganing down the hill at speed! Getting back up again was a different story. *(Win Haines)*

87 and **88**   During four summers between 1894 and 1898 the farm labourer, Harry Toyer, visited Russia.   It is said that he went to learn farming, but this country boy, raised in Lilley, spoke no Russian.   It is possible that he attended one of the farming Colleges that existed in Imperial Russia at that time.   Who paid for him and how did he communicate? Even his daughters could not answer this question.   He lived near St Petersburg and his passport still exists.   When he returned, he married and worked for the rest of his life at Manor Farm.   The lower picture shows him on a sleigh.   *(Author's Collection)*

89 A feature of Bradgers Hill and the countryside around Stopsley before the War were the threatening *Trespassers will be Prosecuted* notices. Set up by landowners jealously guarding their properties and wary of poachers, they were seen by local lads like Ray Miller as a symbol of authority to be defied. There was usually a gamekeeper not far away. Behind the sign Common Farm can just be seen. A Sale notice of 1846 suggests that Bradgers Hill is a corruption of Bradshaw's Hill. *(Freda Pinney)*

90 This colourful character was known as 'Nimrod' Stevens. He lived in a cottage in 'the dell' in St Thomas' Road (No's 38-42). It is said that he liked to hide in trees, jump out on children and chase them. It is also alleged that he stalked young ladies, walking five paces behind them, and claiming that he was only seeing them safely home. It is doubtful if he would have been tolerated in Stopsley today. *(Josie Driscoll)*

91   Nurse Molyneux was Stopsley's District Nurse in the 1930s.   She was very popular with younger children, and is remembered for giving them sugar mice if they did not cry whilst being treated.   *(Josie Driscoll)*

92   The Stopsley Day Nursery opened on 27th October 1944, and its first Matron was Joan Hadfield (left), seen here with Sister Price. Miss Hadfield ran the Nursery for 19 years until July 1963.   Mrs Price succeeded her for ten months, until Mrs Norwood was appointed in September 1964. From 1969 until 1994 Mrs Payne was the Matron. *(Maureen Bland)*

93 Sir Francis Cassel inherited the Putteridge Bury estate in 1953, and lived in a house near the Stopsley entrance to the park. He was a talented pianist who gave concerts all over Europe. In his later years he became a succesful owner of race horses which he kept on the estate. He died in 1967. *(Cassel family)*

94 Florence Cox was the wife of John Cox, the grocer, who moved to 617 Hitchin Road, Stopsley, from Park Street in 1935. Apart from helping to run the shop, she was a well-respected member of St Thomas' Church serving on the Parochial Church Council and numerous other committees. She is seen here in 1973, knitting blankets for the Red Cross. With her is Rene Knight, another indefatigable worker for the church and St John Ambulance. *(Myrtle Cox)*

95 Gertrude Clarke was the much respected Headmistress of Stopsley Infant School from 1920 to 1942. She is seen here in the boys' playground, with the house of William Hill (sexton and verger) behind. Les Church recalls that Mrs Hill objected to boys kicking balls into her garden and would not return them, putting them onto her wash-house fire instead. One day the boys put a firework into a ball and deliberately kicked it into the garden. Shortly afterwards there was a loud explosion from the wash-house. Mrs Hill did not burn any more balls! *(Ethel Toyer)*

96 Tom Whalley was the popular Headmaster of Stopsley Senior School from 1925 to 1940. The Senior School occupied the greater part of the present Infant School and became grossly overcrowded, having been built to house 158 children and by 1938 taking 339! Discipline broke down and a 'hit squad' of three mature teachers: Harry Simpson, Mabel Knight and Mr I. Fern, were moved in. Tom Whalley was made a scapegoat by the local education authority for problems that were not of his making. He chose not to apply for the Headship of the new Stopsley School (present Juniors) when it opened in 1940.

(R.D.Whalley)

97 Harry J. Dawe was the first Headmaster of Stopsley Secondary Modern Boys' School when it opened on 7th September 1948. Built on the site of Bury Farm in St Thomas' Road, the early school utilised some of the old farm stables for classrooms, and animals were kept in others as part of the popular Rural Science course. Amongst Mr Dawe's pupils at the school in 1950 was the actor Rodney Bewes of *The Likely Lads* television fame.

98 Mary A. Millen was appointed Headmistress of Stopsley Secondary Modern Girls' School which opened on 31st January 1949. She instantly walked into a dispute with the Vicar, Revd. H. T. Pimm, who had barred the Girl Guides (amongst others) from meeting in the Church Institute. The Guides re-formed at the school, and the Vicar attempted to freeze their assets, claiming they were only for a church group. He eventually reached agreement with the County Commissioner to give the school half the funds. Miss Millen showed her displeasure by declining to accept them!

99 From 1920 Ethel Toyer worked as a monitoress under Charles Breed, and from 1922 as a student teacher under Gertrude Clarke at Stopsley Infant School. She completed a long career in teaching at Lilley School. The eldest of Harry Toyer's three daughters (see 86), she was always of an enquiring nature, and took many Box-Brownie snapshots of Stopsley during the late 20s and 30s. One of her most enduring photos shows a blank sky above her home in Wigmore Lane. Her caption reads: 'The view from our garden, just *after* the R101 airship had passed over'! *(Author's Colln)*

100 In September 1960 Cedric William Griggs was appointed Ramridge Junior School's second Headteacher. He had a formidable reputation locally and nationally as a J.P. and Chairman of Magistrates, a member of the Burnham Committee (on teachers' salaries) and the Schools' Broadcasting Council. It was in his school and the classroom that Cedric Griggs was happiest. He was a brilliant teacher, and although he was very firm (but fair), the children loved him and under his care Ramridge became a highly respected Junior School. He retired in 1971. *(Luton News)*

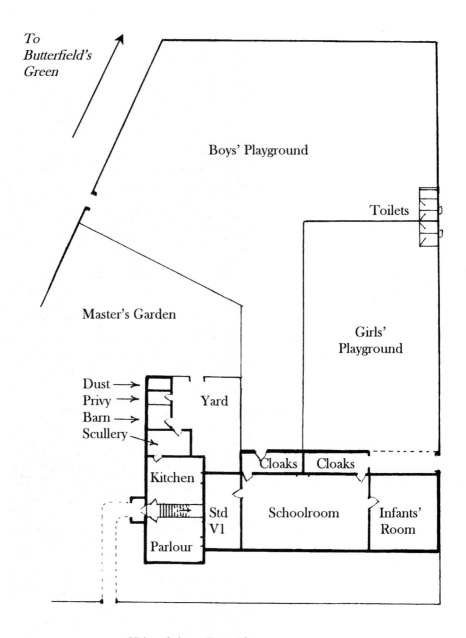

To Butterfield's Green

Boys' Playground

Toilets

Master's Garden

Girls' Playground

Dust →
Privy →
Barn →
Scullery →

Yard

Cloaks   Cloaks

Kitchen

Std
V1

Schoolroom

Infants'
Room

Parlour

Hitchin   Road

101 A plan of the Stopsley National School at Swift's Green (at the entrance to Butterfield's Green Road), built in 1858. The plan is based on that of the architect H. Holgate, with some additional information from the late Walter Lawrence. At first the toilets were too close to the school and had to be moved to the position shown on this plan in 1887. They emptied directly into a dumbwell, which in June 1899 had not been emptied for two years! The Log Book records that the smell was fearfull! The Infants' Room with tiered seating was added in 1889, and the cloakrooms enlarged in 1899. Outside the girls' entrance was a covered area where lessons were held in summer. There was no tap water supply until July 1906.

102 This photograph shows the old School covered in snow, about 1925. The lower roof of the infant classroom added in 1889 can be clearly seen, as can the chimney of the ventilator. Although the School closed in 1912, Charles Breed, the Headmaster, continued to live in the School House until his death in 1954. The remainder of the building was used by the Church as a meeting room for a variety of activities. During the 2nd World War it was the local headquarters of the Civil Defence, and was afterwards used for emergency housing. It was demolished in 1956. *(William Lockey)*

103 An infant class at the old School in the summer of 1901. Charles Breed stands on the right, and the lady teachers are probably Myra Landricome, Edith Brown and Lily Tompkins. Although the children are dressed in their best clothes for the photograph, it is clear that poverty was rife in most of their homes. One little boy (holding the board) is wearing glasses. Fourteen years later most of these boys would be at the War. *(Author's Collection)*

104 At the side of the new village School in 1914. Mr Breed stands with a class of older children. On the left are teachers Nellie Mantz and Gertrude Hucklesby. The pupil teacher on the right is Dorothy Thorne (aged 14). The window on the right has been replaced by a door. *(Author's Collection)*

105 The infant class of 1914 photographed in the front playground of the new School looking towards the Green. Charlotte Nott, the Headmistress, is with the children. Norman Fisher (see plate 1) is third from the left in the back row. On the whole the children look more prosperous than those of 1901. *(Josie Driscoll)*

106 The staff of the Senior School in 1914. At the back are Dorothy Thorne, daughter of the Head Gardener at Putteridge Bury, and Mrs Florence King. Miss Nellie Mantz, Charles Breed and Miss Gertrude Hucklesby are seated. Jock, the school dog and rodent control officer, is in the foreground! *(Author's Collection)*

107 Teacher, Albert 'Billy' Williams and boys from his class on their way to watch the local Coronation procession through Luton on 12th May, 1937. The long walk was worth it as there was a free tea in Pope's Meadow afterwards. The boys in the picture include Evelyn Shaw, Alec Church, Charlie Hall, Ted Dumpleton, Dick Robinson, Geof Smith and Jack Saunders. *(Author's Collection)*

108 The school that opened in Stopsley in September 1940 had the distinction of being the only new one in England to be opened during the War.   Its large windows were designed to admit maximum light and air, part of a government initiative to help eradicate tuberculosis in young children.   Unfortunately, the possibility of flying glass was a major hazard when air raids were expected daily, and safety net had to be pasted over all the windows. *(James Dyer)*

109 Stopsley Council School was officially opened on Thursday, 19th September, 1940 by the President of the Association of Education Committees, George Tomlinson MP, in the presence of the Mayor of Luton, Councillor John Burgoyne.   They are seen here with the Headmaster Leonard Benson (left) and the former Headmaster, Charles Breed. *(Luton News)*

110 This snapshot of the Stopsley Council School staff was taken in 1946. The men in the back row are Ivor David and Mr Hodges, whilst at the front are Hilda Kiddy, Mabel Knight, Leonard Benson, Winifred Froud and Miss Samuels. *(Hillary Stubbs)*

111 The senior boys' class at the Council School performed their version of *A Christmas Carol* on 16th December, 1947. Produced by Ivor Moyle, the actors were Richard Jenkins, Walter Rainbow, Brian Bulpitt, Brian Watts and Ronald Chamberlain. The old wooden desk in the photograph had been in the school since it opened in 1858. *(Luton News)*

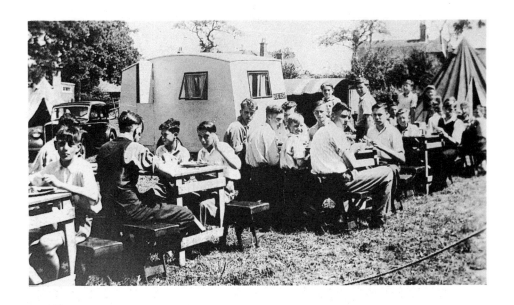

112 and **113** Present and former pupils from Stopsley Council School enjoyed a Harvest Camp at Northian, near Rye in Sussex, beginning on 18th July, 1947. The Headmaster, teachers and parents accompanied the lads, who picked fruit for three weeks as part of a government sponsored project to 'lend a hand on the land'. Amongst those in the lower picture are Ronald Chamberlain, Philip Kime, Douglas Dann, George Adams and Jack Fensome. *(Tilly Hodgson)*

114 By February 1949 all the senior pupils had moved from Stopsley Council School to the new Secondary Schools in St Thomas' Road.   The School that remained became Stopsley Junior School and these parents are watching its first Sports Day on 22nd June, 1949.   It was held in the Ashcroft Road Recreation Ground.   The bank covering one of the former air raid shelters can be seen in the background, its entrances screened by chestnut fencing.

(Luton News)

115 The Headmaster, Leonard Benson, announces the results of another Sports Day on 19th May, 1954.   Lesley Roylance and John Fahy, the Captains of Montgomery House, await the presentation of the House Shield.   The young *Luton News* reporter on the right is former Luton Grammar School boy, Ian Brodie.   Today he is *The Times* correspondent in Washington, USA.   *(Stopsley Junior School Archives)*

116 The last class of senior girls from Stopsley Council School, visiting *Madame Tussauds* at Christmas 1947. As this visit is not recorded in the School Log Book it seems likely that it was privately arranged by Winifred Froud, their class teacher. School visits could be organised with the minimum of red tape in those halcyon days!

117 This happy picture was taken at the Junior School Harvest Festival on 22nd September, 1950. At that time all the older children had their own school garden plots where they grew a variety of crops as part of the rural science syllabus. After the proceedings "masses of vegetables, fruit and flowers were transported to the Children's (London Road) and Alexandra Hospitals". The lads with the potatoes are John Green, Tom Slender and Malcolm Meldrum. *(Luton News)*

118 During the summer of 1956 the Junior School took delivery of new Wicksteed climbing apparatus for physical education.   Its positioning above an asphalt playground led to a number of nasty accidents and it would not be sanctioned today.   In 1954 accommodation in the school was stretched to its limit with 800 pupils.   Some of the hutted classrooms built to help alleviate the problem are seen in the background.   Matters were eased considerably when Ramridge Junior School opened in January 1955.   *(Wicksteeds)*

119   On 15th and 16th December 1952 Stopsley Junior School presented two performances of a lavish pantomime called *Sinbad*.   The School *Log Book* does not record the details, but the cast was enormous: not surprising, perhaps, with 710 pupils to choose from at that time.

(Luton News)

120 In 1948-49 and 1949-50 Stopsley School were the Junior League Champions for two years in succession. Their success was due in no small part to the presence of two sets of Bowler twins in the first season. *Back row*: J. Stevens, James Bowler, Jack Lindsay, B. Wakelin, R. Standring, Alan Kidd. *Seated:* G. Lambert, Nicholas Morrissey, John Bowler, David Hetherington, C. Hyde. *Front:* Peter Bowler, Paul Bowler. (Jack Lindsay has achieved fame as trainer of the boxer, Billy Schwer). *(School Archives)*

121 The 1949-50 League Champions: *Back Row:* R. Watt, Peter Bowler, G. Barton, P. Early, E. Threader, G. Fahy, Paul Bowler. *Front Row:* B. Hill, G. Lambert, David Hetherington, A. Thomas, R. Dann. *(School Archives)*

122 Stopsley Youth Council held a May Day festival in Ashcroft Road Recreation Ground in 1943.   It was intended to boost the morale of Stopsley folk during the third year of the War. Here the 11th Luton Girls' Brigade are performing in the rain, watched by the May Queen, Fay Fryer, in the background.   The Revd. Alan Funnell and event organiser George Souster stroll past the proceedings.   *(Luton News)*

123   Stopsley Brownies taking part in a skipping display in the Junior School playground in 1946.   The girls include June Knight, Mary Witney, Ann Britten, Betty Bodsworth, Josie Fisher and Gillian Hodgson.   *(Josie Driscoll)*

124 I.T.A. film cameras were at Stopsley Secondary Modern School for one hectic week early in 1964. They were making a programme called *Learning for Life*, part of a television series on Citizenship. In this shot from the film, teacher Colin Burnham is discussing a topic with Peter Keller. The school was paid £50 for taking part. *(A.B.C. TV)*

125 In 1960 the orchestral Conductor, Sir Malcolm Sargent, gave Stopsley S.M. School permission to name a school House after him. A happy relationship grew up between members of the House and Sir Malcolm, and after his death on 4th October, 1967 the school was represented at his memorial service. Early in 1968 a specially commissioned bronze relief plaque was unveiled to Sir Malcolm's memory at the school. Headmaster, Dr Walter Roy is seen here with the distinguished sculptress Dora Barrett, who undertook the work, and Norman Nash, the House Master. *(Luton News: Luton Museum Collection)*

126 Ashcoft Secondary Modern Girls' School opened in September 1960 to cater for girls in south Stopsley. The Headmistress was Dorothy Briggs. Boys continued to go to Stopsley S.M. School until the late 1960s. This photograph, taken at the time of the school's opening, shows girls demonstrating the apparatus in the new gymnasium. *(Luton Education Committee)*

127 At Christmas 1962 the Ashcroft School girls performed two plays, *Treasure Island* and *The Water Gypsies*, seen here. *(Luton News)*

128 As part of Ashcroft School's innovative Homecraft Course, senior girls visited local playgroups and worked with small children. In March 1964 toddlers were invited to the school, where the girls had prepared an appropriate meal for them. *(Luton News)*

129 Ashcroft became a Comprehensive School in 1966, when boys were admitted, one year at a time. In April 1968 these (Year 8) boys won the Luton Schools' Cross-Country Trophy. *Back row:* John Burr, Peter Bostock, Philip Brunton. *Front row:* Stuart Lydon, Peter Howlett, Ernest Wilkins, Brian McCormick, Peter Arthur, Adrian Stearn. *(Luton News)*

130 In October 1968, Miss Alice Bradshaw, formerly Head of History at Ashcroft School, returned to present merit badges to some of her former pupils. *(Luton News)*

131 Some of the children at Someries Junior School were so incensed by the Millwall Football Club riots in 1985 that they sat down to work out their own football supporters' code of conduct. It was published in the local and national press, and the children are pictured here with Headmaster, Louis Fidge, and Form teacher, David Barrick. *(Luton News: Luton Museum Collection)*

132 and **133** Ellen Barber opened her popular 'Tiny Folks' Kindergarten' in Turner's Road in September 1938. Using the Montessori methods of child-centred learning, it gave many local children a firm foundation for their future education. In the lower picture, taken in 1940, Miss Barber is sitting with the children beside the pool which often featured in her nature study work. The Barber family came to Ramridge End Farm from Biggleswade in the 1800s, spreading to Green Farm and Mixes Hill by the beginning of the 20th century.

(William Lockey)

134 A street party held to celebrate Victory in Europe (VE) Day in May 1945. This one was held in Stapleford Road, and amongst those enjoying themselves are Maureen, Roy and Vic Bettis, Howell Thomas, John and Catherine Burke, Arthur and Maureen Draper, Pat Faulkner and Mr Copley. *(Luton News)*

135 The choir of the Sacred Heart Church in Ashcroft Road, taken fairly soon after it opened in November 1950. *Back row:* Mr McIlroy (Jnr.), - , Mr Foley, Mr Cregan, Mr Patterson, Mr Mellor. *Centre row:* Joan Cregan, Mrs Smith, - , - , - , - , May Burke, Mrs Reynolds. *Front row:* Mrs Money, Mrs Morrisey, Mrs Fahy, Father George Walker, Mr McIlroy (Snr.) Choirmaster, Mrs McGarry, Mrs Anderson, Mrs Alderson. *(Luton News)*

136 A VE Day party in Ashcroft Road on 9th May 1945. The children at the table are Stella Cowland, Roger and Molly Clements and Ann Dyer. Behind them are Mrs Cowland and Mrs Goodship. Ted Summerfield stands at the front, and to his left are Miss Wagstaff and Mr Goodship. After five years of austerity there was a feeling that now the Stopsley of pre-war days would return. Nothing could have been further from the truth, Food and clothes continued to be rationed and in short supply. Many men remained in the forces for another year or two before demobilisation. Women, who had done mens' work during the War, and had tasted an alternative to the routine of domestic life, now sought employment in a host of industries that had previously be closed to them. A massive building programme was to alter the face of the countryside for ever, devouring farms and fields and hedgerows. In twenty years the rural village of Stopsley would be buried under miles of tarmac, creating the indifferent suburbia of the late 20th century. *(Frederick Dyer)*

137 The view from the top of Beech Hill on the road to Hitchin, about 1930. Snow covers the fields as the camera looks down towards Lilley Church. On the right is the wall around Putteridge Park. In May 1967 the trees were felled and the road from the county boundary into Stopsley was converted into a dual carriageway at a cost of £90,000. *(William Lockey)*

138 The gates and North Lodge of Putteridge Park about 1930. This was the main entrance to Putteridge Bury, at that time occupied by Sir Felix and Lady Helen Cassel. King George Vth was an occasional visitor, attracted by the pheasant shooting. The Bury was bought by Luton County Borough Council in 1964 for use as a Teacher Training College. Today it is the jewel amongst the properties belonging to the University of Luton. The grounds of the Park remain in private ownership. *(William Lockey)*

139   By the 1960s almost every available piece of land that could be acquired was swallowed-up for building.   The Cassel family disposed of most of their land in Stopsley. By 1967 Rogate Road on the Cassel Park estate was well under construction.   *(James Dyer)*

140 The motor-car, the scourge of the countryside, was extremely popular by the 1930s.   For those who could afford one, it opened up a new world of travel and convenience.   For the local farmers and tradesmen it meant the replacement of their horse-drawn delivery carts with faster motorised vehicles.   In this photograph, farmer Fred Holdstock and his milk delivery man have decorated their Morris milk-van for the 1937 Coronation procession through Luton. *(William Lockey)*

141 and **142** More houses and a vastly increased population put great pressure on local amenities such as water supply and sewage disposal. In the oldest parts of Stopsley, like St Thomas' Road, it became necessary to replace the overloaded sewers, originally laid in 1936. This caused traffic disruption for a few weeks in 1964, but it ensured that the system could cope with the increase in effluent from the Municipal Caravan site and Stopsley High School. *(Colin Nye)*

143 The young men of the Stopsley and District Football Team of 1920-21 played on Smith's Meadow, near Greenways. Unfortunately their names are not recorded although the man at the left end of the back row is Teddy Martin, who lived in a house by the Green. He was a barber who travelled from house to house charging tuppence (1p.) for a haircut. He always carried his scissors and razors with him in his little white box.

144 The Ashcroft Juniors (Stopsley) F.C. Team of 1938-39 were the first to play in the new Ashcroft Road Recreation Ground. *Back row:* Jack Overhill, Ray Miller, Alan Hinksman, Reg Sanders, Albert Ward, John Chamberlain, Bill Swain. *Front row:* Les Church, Jack Thomas, Derek Horton, Bill Sanders, John Lovell. John Chamberlain and Derek Horton died in 1941 and 1943 respectively, as prisoners of the Japanese during World War II.

145 Stopsley's first post-war football team photographed at Butterfield's Green during the 1950-51 season. *Standing:* Les Giltrow, Danny O'Donnell, Roy Butcher, Jim Prudden, Alan Gibbs, Sidney Millen, Tom Adair, Jim Oliver, Gordon Brown, Bill Greenwood. *Seated:* Bert Cumberland, Les Davey, Billy Pugh, Bill Weston, Ron Walker, Jack Horn, Jack Groom (trainer). *(Luton News)*

146 Stopsley Cricket Club re-formed in 1947 at Lothair Road, where a wooden pavilion was shared with the footballers. This is the Stopsley team of 1949. *Standing:* Jack Groom, Alan Gibbs, Dick Inkpen, Curly Cook, Ron Waller, Stan Coleman, Joe Deamer, Les Waller. *Seated:* Harry Monty, Bill Walker, Jack Schatten, Ernie Hill, Ernie Reid. *Front:* Brin Griffiths, Arthur Gunner. *(Luton News)*

147 The Ashcroft Road Recreation Ground opened in 1938. One of its more attractive features was the paddling pool with its central fountain. Unfortunately the smooth floor of the pool attracted an unpleasant green algae which made it very slippery. Early in the War it was drained as a precaution against poliomyelitis. It was seasonally opened again for short periods in the late 1950s. This photo is from 1957. *(Basil Cheverton)*

148 The author tries out the drinking fountain in the Ashcroft Road 'Rec' about 1940. If you placed your finger in the right position you could squirt water all over your companions! The decorative shrubs that were to line the entrance drive, and provide a splendid place to play hide-and-seek, had not been planted at this time. *(Frederick Dyer)*

149 *The Brickmaker's Arms* in St Thomas' Road in 1985. It had begun trading by the 1860s. In 1910 it opened from 6am until midnight, as did the other Stopsley pubs. Almost ninety years later, trade had declined so much that its owners, Whitbread, closed it in 1997 and it was demolished in the following year. Houses, and bungalows named St Thomas' Court, were built on the site in 1999. *(Alan Thayne)*

150 The rear of *The Brickmaker's Arms* in 1989. The large room on the left was added in the 1930s and used for social activities and wedding receptions. It replaced a well-stocked rose garden created by George Bennett, publican in the 1920s. *(Alan Thayne)*

151 *The First and Last* in 1972, with the edge of *Stopsley House* on the right. One of Stopsley's most popular public houses, it began trading about 1868, but with declining trade its last owners, Whitbread, closed it in 1997. It has been the Luton Conservative Social Club since 1998. *Stopsley House* was the home of the Allen family, before becoming the home and surgery of successive GPs, Drs. Anderson and Garrett. *(James Dyer)*

 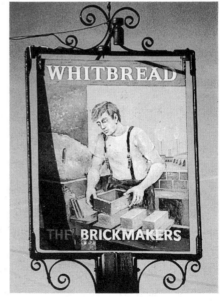

152 and **153** Signs from Stopsley's two closed public houses, *The First and Last* and *The Brickmaker's Arms*. The former has been variously interpreted as the first and last drink of the day, or the first and last pub when travelling through the village. The latter illustrates the production of hand-made bricks in the St Thomas' Road brickworks. The *Arms* referred to the armorial bearings of the Brickmakers' Company. *(James Dyer)*

155 During the 1930s the northern end of *Tithe Cottage* was demolished and a new wing was added on the south. This became the Greenways Café and Filling Station (photographed in 1959) and a popular 'pull-in' for lorry drivers heading to and from the east coast. The house was demolished in 1963 when a new filling station shared the site with the Lee-West Bowling Alley. The latter burned down in somewhat mysterious circumstances on 9th March 1967. *(Bob Norman)*

154 *The Sportsman* is Stopsley's oldest public house, and the only one to survive in the historic centre of the parish. The earliest record is in a *Directory* of 1839 which lists James Darley as the innkeeper. In the 19th century Mardall's of Harpenden were the brewers, until they were bought out by Glover and Sons (also of Harpenden). In 1919 the Luton firm of J. W. Green acquired the property. In 1962, like the other village centre pubs, it was acquired by Whitbread's. *(James Dyer)*

156   Cottages beside the Green (No's 623-631) in 1962.   These were all demolished to make way for the enlargement of the Petrol Station forecourt.   An alleyway known as Harris Lane, which led through to Lothair Road and the fields beyond, passed between the white cottages.   *(James Dyer)*

157   The interior of Stopsley Library before its refurbishment in 1994, with the Librarian, Mary Wilson, date-stamping a customer's book and filing her borrower's ticket.   The Library is an essential part of the cultural life of Stopsley, providing a most valuable service for all sections of the community, and in particular for the very young and the elderly.

Index

of Plate Numbers

Books Published by
THE BOOK CASTLE

COUNTRYSIDE CYCLING IN BEDFORDSHIRE, BUCKINGHAMSHIRE AND HERTFORDSHIRE: Mick Payne. Twenty rides on- and off-road for all the family.

PUB WALKS FROM COUNTRY STATIONS: Bedfordshire and Hertfordshire: Clive Higgs. Fourteen circular country rambles, each starting and finishing at a railway station and incorporating a pub-stop at a mid-way point.

PUB WALKS FROM COUNTRY STATIONS: Buckinghamshire and Oxfordshire: Clive Higgs. Circular rambles incorporating pub-stops.

LOCAL WALKS: South Bedfordshire and North Chilterns: Vaughan Basham. Twenty-seven thematic circular walks.

LOCAL WALKS: North and Mid Bedfordshire: Vaughan Basham. Twenty-five thematic circular walks.

FAMILY WALKS: Chilterns South: Nick Moon. Thirty 3 to 5 mile circular walks.

FAMILY WALKS: Chilterns North: Nick Moon. Thirty shorter circular walks.

CHILTERN WALKS: Hertfordshire, Bedfordshire and North Buckinghamshire: Nick Moon.

CHILTERN WALKS: Buckinghamshire: Nick Moon.

CHILTERN WALKS: Oxfordshire and West Buckinghamshire: Nick Moon.
A trilogy of circular walks, in association with the Chiltern Society.
Each volume contains 30 circular walks.

OXFORDSHIRE WALKS: Oxford, the Cotswolds and the Cherwell Valley: Nick Moon.

OXFORDSHIRE WALKS: Oxford, the Downs and the Thames Valley: Nick Moon.
Two volumes that complement Chiltern Walks: Oxfordshire and complete coverage of the county, in association with the Oxford Fieldpaths Society. Thirty circular walks in each.

THE D'ARCY DALTON WAY: Nick Moon.
Long-distance footpath across the Oxfordshire Cotswolds and Thames Valley, with various circular walk suggestions.

JOURNEYS INTO BEDFORDSHIRE: Anthony Mackay.
Foreword by The Marquess of Tavistock, Woburn Abbey. A lavish book of over 150 evocative ink drawings.

JOURNEYS INTO BUCKINGHAMSHIRE: Anthony Mackay
Superb line drawings plus background text: large format landscape gift book.

BUCKINGHAMSHIRE MURDERS: Len Woodley.
Nearly two centuries of nasty crimes.

WINGRAVE: A Rothschild Village in the Vale: Margaret and Ken Morley.
Thoroughly researched and copiously illustrated survey of the last 200 years in this lovely village between Aylesbury and Leighton Buzzard.

HISTORIC FIGURES IN THE BUCKINGHAMSHIRE LANDSCAPE: John Houghton.
Major personalities and events that have shaped the county's past, including a special section on Bletchley Park.

TWICE UPON A TIME: John Houghton.
Short stories loosely based on fact, set in the North Bucks area.

MANORS and MAYHEM, PAUPERS and PARSONS:
Tales from Four Shires: Beds., Bucks., Herts., and Northants.: John Houghton
Little-known historical snippets and stories.

MYTHS and WITCHES, PEOPLE and POLITICS:
Tales from Four Shires: Bucks., Beds., Herts., and Northants.: John Houghton.
Anthology of strange, but true historical events.

FOLK: Characters and Events in the History of Bedfordshire and Northamptonshire:
Vivienne Evans. Anthology about people of yesteryear – arranged alphabetically by village or town.

JOHN BUNYAN: His Life and Times: Vivienne Evans.
Highly-praised and readable account.

THE RAILWAY AGE IN BEDFORDSHIRE: Fred Cockman.
Classic, illustrated account of early railway history.
A LASTING IMPRESSION: Michael Dundrow.
A boyhood evacuee recalls his years in the Chiltern village of Totternhoe near Dunstable.
GLEANINGS REVISITED: Nostalgic Thoughts of a Bedfordshire Farmer's Boy: E W O'Dell.
His own sketches and early photographs adorn this lively account of rural Bedfordshire in days gone by.
BEDFORDSHIRE'S YESTERYEARS Vol 2: The Rural Scene: Brenda Fraser-Newstead.
Vivid first-hand accounts of country life two or three generations ago.
BEDFORDSHIRE'S YESTERYEARS Vol 3: Craftsmen and Tradespeople:
Brenda Fraser-Newstead.
Fascinating recollections over several generations practising many vanishing crafts and trades.
BEDFORDSHIRE'S YESTERYEARS Vol 4: War Times and Civil Matters:
Brenda Fraser-Newstead.
Two World Wars, plus transport, law and order, etc.
PROUD HERITAGE: A Brief History of Dunstable, 1000–2000AD: Vivienne Evans.
Century by century account of the town's rich tradition and key events, many of national significance.
DUNSTABLE WITH THE PRIORY: 1100–1550: Vivienne Evans.
Dramatic growth of Henry I's important new town around a major crossroads.
DUNSTABLE IN TRANSITION: 1550–1700: Vivienne Evans.
Wealth of original material as the town evolves without the Priory.
DUNSTABLE DECADE: THE EIGHTIES: A Collection of Photographs: Pat Lovering.
A souvenir book of nearly 300 pictures of people and events in the 1980s.
STREETS AHEAD: An Illustrated Guide to the Origins of Dunstable's Street Names:
Richard Walden.
Fascinating text and captions to hundreds of photographs, past and present, throughout the town.
DUNSTABLE IN DETAIL: Nigel Benson.
A hundred of the town's buildings and features, plus town trail map.
OLD DUNSTABLE: Bill Twaddle.
A new edition of this collection of early photographs.
BOURNE and BRED: A Dunstable Boyhood Between the Wars: Colin Bourne.
An elegantly written, well-illustrated book capturing the spirit of the town over fifty years ago.
ROYAL HOUGHTON: Pat Lovering:
Illustrated history of Houghton Regis from the earliest times to the present.
THE STOPSLEY BOOK: James Dyer.
Definitive, detailed account of this historic area of Luton. 150 rare photographs.
THE STOPSLEY PICTURE BOOK: James Dyer.
New material and photographs make an ideal companion to The Stopsley Book.
PUBS and PINTS: The Story of Luton's Public Houses and Breweries: Stuart Smith.
The background to beer in the town, plus hundreds of photographs, old and new.
THE CHANGING FACE OF LUTON: An Illustrated History:
Stephen Bunker, Robin Holgate and Marian Nichols. Luton's development from earliest times to
the present busy industrial town. Illustrated in colour and mono.
WHERE THEY BURNT THE TOWN HALL DOWN:
Luton, The First World War and the Peace Day Riots, July 1919: Dave Craddock.
Detailed analysis of a notorious incident.
THE MEN WHO WORE STRAW HELMETS: Policing Luton, 1840–1974: Tom Madigan.
Meticulously chronicled history; dozens of rare photographs; author served in Luton Police for
fifty years.
BETWEEN THE HILLS: The Story of Lilley, a Chiltern Village: Roy Pinnock.
A priceless piece of our heritage – the rural beauty remains but the customs and way of life
described here have largely disappeared.
KENILWORTH SUNSET: A Luton Town Supporter's Journal: Tim Kingston.
Frank and funny account of football's ups and downs.
A HATTER GOES MAD!: Kristina Howells.
Luton Town footballers, officials and supporters talk to a female fan.

LEGACIES: Tales and Legends of Luton and the North Chilterns: Vic Lea.
Twenty-five mysteries and stories based on fact, including Luton Town Football Club. Many photographs.

THREADS OF TIME: Shela Porter.
The life of a remarkable mother and businesswoman, spanning the entire century and based in Hitchin and (mainly) Bedford.

LEAFING THROUGH LITERATURE:
Writers' Lives in Hertfordshire and Bedfordshire: David Carroll.
Illustrated short biographies of many famous authors and their connections with these counties.

A PILGRIMAGE IN HERTFORDSHIRE: H M Alderman.
Classic, between-the-wars tour round the county, embellished with line drawings.

THE VALE OF THE NIGHTINGALE: Molly Andrews.
Several generations of a family, lived against a Harpenden backdrop.

SUGAR MICE AND STICKLEBACKS:
Childhood Memories of a Hertfordshire Lad: Harry Edwards
Vivid evocation of those gentler pre-war days in an archetypal village, Hertingfordbury.

SWANS IN MY KITCHEN: Lis Dorer.
Story of a Swan Sanctuary near Hemel Hempstead.

THE HILL OF THE MARTYR: An Architectural History of St. Albans Abbey: Eileen Roberts.
Scholarly and readable chronological narrative history of Hertfordshire and Bedfordshire's famous cathedral. Fully illustrated with photographs and plans.

CHILTERN ARCHAEOLOGY: RECENT WORK: A Handbook for the Next Decade:
edited by Robin Holgate. The latest views, results and excavations by twenty-three leading archaeologists throughout the Chilterns.

THE TALL HITCHIN INSPECTOR'S CASEBOOK:
A Victorian Crime Novel Based on Fact: Edgar Newman.
Worthies of the time encounter more archetypal villains.

SPECIALLY FOR CHILDREN

VILLA BELOW THE KNOLLS: A Story of Roman Britain: Michael Dundrow.
An exciting adventure for young John in Totternhoe and Dunstable two thousand years ago.

THE RAVENS: One Boy Against the Might of Rome: James Dyer.
On the Barton Hills and in the south-east of England as the men of the great fort of Ravensburgh (near Hexton) confront the invaders.

Books Distributed by THE BOOK CASTLE

Pictorial Guide to Bedfordshire .... Meadows / Larkman
The Story of Bedford .... Godber
Pictorial Guide to Hertfordshire .... Meadows
The Story of St. Albans .... Toms
History of Milton Keynes, vol 1 .... Markham
History of Milton Keynes, vol 2 .... Markham
Old Aylesbury .... Viney / Nightingale
Village Schooldays and Beyond, 1906–23 .... Chapman
Claydon .... Chapman

Further titles are in preparation.
All the above are available via any bookshop, or from the publisher and bookseller,
THE BOOK CASTLE
12 Church Street Dunstable, Bedfordshire, LU5 4RU
Tel: (01582) 605670